First published in 2006 by
Sutton Publishing Limited . Phoenix Mill
Thrupp . Stroud . Gloucestershire . GL5 2BU

Reprinted 2006

British Library Cataloguing in Publication Data
A catalogue record for this book is available from the British Library.

ISBN 0-7509-4532-X

Title page: The author examines his favourite vintage sports car, one of Lionel Martin's superbly engineered Aston-Martins. This car, chassis 1944, is the property of John Milner, seen here. *(Mrs A. Milner)*

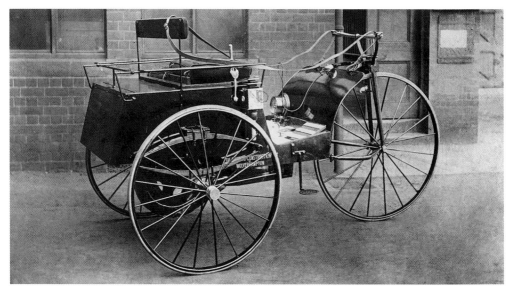

A primitive: this is an electric dog-cart built by Tom Parker of the Electrical Construction Company, Wolverhampton, *c.* 1888. Steering that large single front wheel by means of reins may have been a sop to the days of the horse but could hardly have produced accuracy. *(Shropshire Libraries)*

Typeset in 10½/13½ pt Photina.
Typesetting and origination by
Sutton Publishing Limited.
Printed and bound in England by
J.H. Haynes & Co. Ltd, Sparkford.

CONTENTS

ACKNOWLEDGEMENTS

The author's archive of motoring photographs has been built up over many years and kind friends and fellow enthusiasts have generously contributed to the collection. Individual photographs are each acknowledged separately. Where no such acknowledgement appears, the photograph had no attribution when found or purchased and has defied further research. Inevitably there will be some errors of omission for which sincere apologies are offered.

The young man here looks very proud of both his car and his young lady. The car is a 1914 Swift light car. Note the bulb horn at rather an odd angle, the electric horn on the running-board and beside it an acetylene generator for the two scuttle lamps.

INTRODUCTION

You never know what's around the corner. This is as true of motoring (in the pre-motorway age) as it is of life. This book aims to take the reader on a photographic journey through every aspect of motoring from 1900 to 1940.

The dawn of the motor age heralded new ideas, a different perspective and, most importantly, social changes. Much of this change had begun more than fifty years earlier with the coming of the railways and the spread of cycling, the latter giving freedom of choice of route and journey time that the railways with their fixed tracks and timetables were unable to match. The motor age extended that freedom of choice. Of course, the old ways didn't change overnight and many, particularly in rural areas, resented change. What might be round that corner – a flooded road, a speed trap, a splendid view, a nasty accident?

This 16hp Bell, made by Bell Brothers of Ravensthorpe, Yorkshire, was owned by Jack Kitchen of Windermere. He was a prolific inventor who in 1904 used a steam launch on the lake for experiments with radio control. The twelve lamps above the screen on this car could be aimed to the roadside or backwards for reversing. *(Windermere Nautical Trust)*

A splendid 30hp Sheffield-Simplex torpedo phaeton of about 1914 has an ample two-piece windscreen and its hood is neatly encased in a hood bag. The ladies make use of shawls to keep their hats in place in the slipstream.

In following our photographic journey you will meet with these and more, observing as you go changes in dress fashion, street furniture and the vehicles on the roads. You will encounter motor sport very prominently, for the challenge it presents has always had a vital part to play in the British psyche. I make no apology for including so much of it, but at least it comes in small doses. I must even confess to having followed British motorists abroad for one reason or another, whether on holiday, in pursuit of sporting achievement or whatever. Thus the spectrum of photographs is wide and includes some different scenery, most of it attractive.

Was it all a bed of roses in those far-off days? By no means. Early cars and motor-cycles were often unreliable, petrol was not always available, road surfaces were usually appalling and punctures frequent. The law was often both harsh and biased. All in all, it is surprising and much to the credit of those motoring pioneers that the motor car of 1914 was streets ahead of its parent of only fourteen years earlier.

The technical demands of the First World War brought about significant advances, the benefits of which would be felt in the years to come. The return of peace brought about new concerns: shortage of materials, industrial unrest and rocketing prices all came into conflict with the insatiable demands of a populace now much more mechanically aware and longing to throw off old restraints and old ways and get on with the new – the 'roaring twenties' indeed.

This 18–24hp De Dietrich phaeton, dark blue, was registered on 1 January 1904 as F 65 to Captain H.W. Calverley of Down Hall, Harlow, Essex. Here it is about to set out on a fine summer's day but leaving the dog at home. The car was sold on 23 June 1906 to Major E.H.J. Parsons, Chief Constable of New Scotland Yard, London. *(J.C. Tarring/E. Salisbury)*

Two major wars in less than half a century were a hard cross to bear. As the 1930s progressed and political instability became more unsettling, so motorists with a sense of impending doom tried to extract the last ounce of pleasure from their pastime, from one last trip with the children to the seaside (the beaches were soon to be off-limits and fortified), from one last race meeting at Brooklands or Shelsley Walsh, and from saying for perhaps the last time, 'Fill her up!' All too soon there would be the blackout, petrol rationing and shortages of all kinds again. All this will be captured in our pictorial journey.

1

The Formative Years
to 1918

Horse-carriage ancestry is still very evident in this Arrol-Johnston dog-cart of about 1900. Note the wooden non-detachable wheels, those at the rear being of larger diameter, the solid rubber tyres and the primitive spoon brake acting on the rear tyres. *(Aberdeen University Library. G.W. Wilson Collection)*

Three Léon-Bollée tricars of the immediately pre-1900 era, with suitably clad occupants. These quaint little three-wheelers were made under licence by a number of British firms, including Humber of Beeston and Coventry. (*Windermere Nautical Trust*)

The 1,000 Miles Trial of 1900, which covered the length and breadth of the country, was the first major event in Britain to make the general public aware of the motor car. Here, passing through Worcester, is the Parisian Daimler owned by Alfred Harmsworth, proprietor of the *Daily Mail*. (*Worcester Record Office*)

In trouble with the law. The driver of this 1902 Lanchester appears to have been caught in a speed trap, a common occurrence in the pioneer days of motoring. *(Mrs Scott)*

Léon Serpollet's steam Serpollet, nicknamed 'Easter Egg', at the Bexhill Speed Trials of 19 July 1902. He put up the fastest time of the day. *(Mrs Scott)*

This 1902 Panhard & Levassor is proving reluctant to start and is occupying everyone's attention and, perhaps, advice. She did start eventually on a fine sunny day . . . *(Mrs Scott)*

. . . She's away, and here poses for a snapshot in the Scottish Highlands. The door of this rear-entrance tonneau is open for the photographer to alight. Note the sprag firmly dug into the ground to prevent the car running backward. *(Mrs Scott)*

Tyre trouble beset this Gardner-Serpollet steam car on its way to Geneva in 1903. The chauffeur, Simpson, is hard at work while the ladies look on. Shortly after this a disaster occurred when the car blew up, laconically recorded as 'wrecked motor'. *(R.J.R. Benson)*

The Gordon Bennett race of 1902 was won by a British car, entitling the 1903 event to be held on British soil. Ireland's more relaxed attitude to the closure of public roads for such a purpose made it the perfect choice. Here Mansfield Cumming is seen at the Moat of Ardscull near Athy with the course car that had raced in the notorious Paris–Madrid race in May 1903.

One of the unsuccessful American Winton racers is fast enough to defeat the photographer at the same location . . .

. . . but he got a slightly sharper image next time round.

This early car pre-dates the requirement to carry a registration number (1904). Observe the beautifully crafted basketwork for small luggage, probably matched by a twin on the other side of the car.

A very early example of a British Daimler, with fixed wooden wheels, solid tyres and tiller steering. Quite what part the horse-drawn fire engine plays in the scene is hard to determine – perhaps it was a practice outing, as they seem not to be in a hurry. *(Mrs Scott)*

In the pioneer years cockpits were exposed and instrumentation was minimal. This 1903 Humberette displays the maker's characteristic single-spoke steering wheel. *(J. Ahern/D. Irvine)*

H.V. Fedden, elder brother of Roy (later Sir Roy) Fedden of Straker-Squire and aviation fame, owned two Bristol cars between 1 April 1904 and 28 July 1904. Here is the first of them, coloured green and registered AE 141. He kept meticulous records of every journey and all work done. Between 1 April and 2 May he covered 586 miles, averaging 14mpg and enjoying thirteen trouble-free days. *(The Revd P. Fedden)*

A one-off. T.J. Biggs had a very varied career, working for several cycle firms, including Raleigh as a draughtsman/designer. Here is his first venture into motor car design, the Eastmead-Biggs car of 1904. He later worked for Humber and Arrol-Johnston, being responsible for several of their major projects. *(Miss K. Biggs)*

Sporting motorists were quick to see the possibilities of racing on the extensive sandy beaches around our coasts. Here in 1904 A. Rawlinson's Gordon-Bennett Darracq and A. Macdonald's impressive Napier are ready for the start at Portmarnock Sands, Ireland.

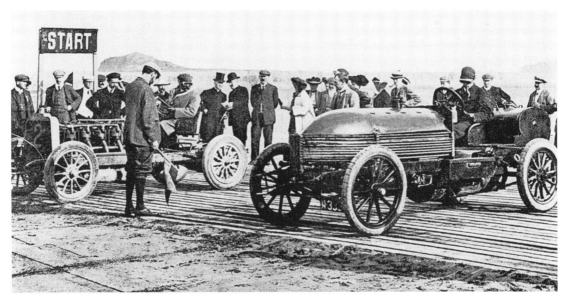

Despite its distinctive appearance I am unable to identify this small car of about 1902, but the dog looks happy enough.

A pioneer lady motorist of note. Dorothy Levett drove large and small cars in many early events. Here her De Dion is on the Bromyard Downs west of Worcester in the 1904 Small Car Trials based in Hereford. The photographer Edmund Williams established the first garage in Bromyard about a quarter of a mile behind the car. *(F. Williams)*

An early and rather primitive Milo forecar of about 1905, a period when vehicles of this type enjoyed a short-lived popularity. These Milo machines were also known by the name of Sharpe but production was very small. *(G.H. Buisst)*

A refreshing halt for this early Decauville and crew at the Waterloo Inn in Bettws. The car was owned in Kidderminster, Worcestershire, when this picture was taken in 1905. *(Midland Automobile Club)*

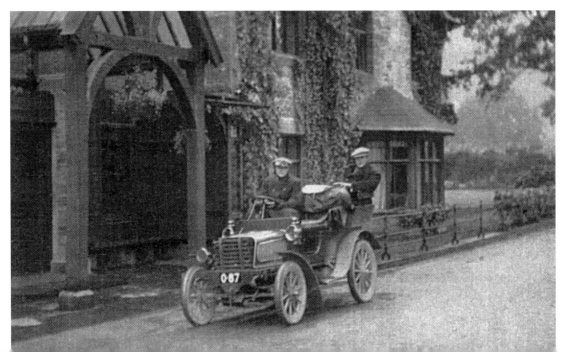

The rebuilt Weir-Darracq that Algernon Lee Guinness entered for the 1905 Eliminating Trials in the Isle of Man. The car was impeccably turned out, as always with Guinness cars, but was eliminated by mechanical troubles.
(S. Hall)

This Shropshire-registered James and Browne (AW 79) was owned by Mrs H. Thursby, resident in that county. The chauffeur is on the left.
(R.J.R. Benson)

An early example, tiller-steered, of the distinctive Lanchester. The car carries the early Derbyshire registration R 16, but . . .

. . . by 1905/6 this number had been transferred to this fine Darracq. The custom of transferring such numbers to a different car in the same ownership was quite common in the early days of motoring.

The owner of the Alldays & Onions lived in Shropshire, hence the AW registration, but it is portrayed here at Colwyn Bay, North Wales. *(R.J.R. Benson)*

Opposite, top: The 100hp racing Darracq raced by 'Algy' Guinness is seen at the start of the Brighton Speed Trials, 1905. *(S. Hall)*

Opposite, bottom: In this pleasant rural scene a single-cylindered 'curved dash' Oldsmobile putters down an unsurfaced road in Herefordshire.

A future prime minister at the wheel, *c.* 1905. Neville Chamberlain takes his family for a trip (quite a long one judging by the luggage) and the servants see them off. The car is a Darracq. *(Mrs M. Simpson)*

Opposite, top: J.A. Doran brings his 22hp Minerva up Shelsley Walsh on 16 June 1905. His time was 220.2s. *(Midland Automobile Club)*

Opposite, bottom: Promenaders! The start of a race in about 1905 on a seaside promenade at Brighton. The cars are (left to right) a 16/20 Mass, 18/24 Gnome (LC 1544) and 20hp MMC (Y 100). *(J. Ahern/D. Irvine)*

Five Edwardian children pose in the smart 1908 Humber in Hallgate, Cottingham, East Yorkshire. (*The Humber Register*)

A smart 16/20 Sunbeam with J.H. and E.J. Bath at Long Wittenham, July 1907. James Henry Bath was a Sunbeam director, whose daughter Olive married Sunbeam's Chief Designer, Louis Coatalen. (*R.J.R. Benson*)

This Minerva, owned by Mr Tomkinson of Kidderminster, is posed at Knightwick in this delightful family snap of about 1907. *(Midland Automobile Club)*

This Minerva has comfortable bodywork with a double-folding front screen and a folding screen for the rear passengers. The ample hood is neatly folded. At this period (*c.* 1909) a crank-handle start was the norm.

FN motorcycles and cars were built by one of Belgium's largest armament makers. This is a 493cc shaft-drive 4-cylinder machine of 1908. The FN motorcycles used shaft-drive transmission exclusively for twenty years from 1903. *(G.D. Smith)*

An obviously posed picture but interesting for all that. The machine is a Premier of about 1910, seemingly in nearly new condition. *(R. Howard)*

Humber machines played an important part in competition between 1903 and 1914. Here is Sam Wright, a works rider, with a 2¾hp V-twin at the Butts cycle track, Coventry, in 1911. *(N. Portway)*

A typical Manx TT scene, with Sam Wright ministering to his latest round-tanked Humber 2¾hp V-twin, 1911. *(N. Portway)*

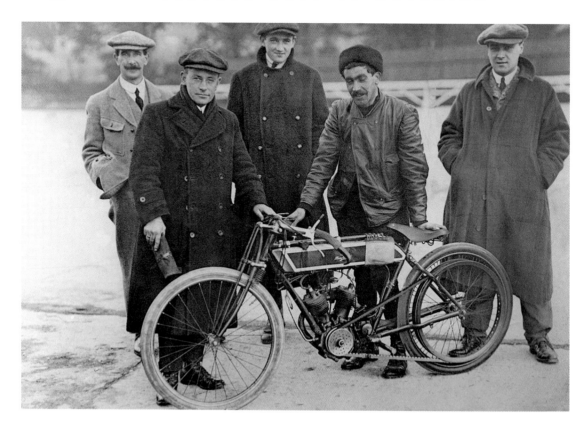

Above: Lady motorcyclist
Mrs Hardee with her 3½hp P&M
bears the scrutiny of the spectators
at the Six Days Trial in 1912.

Right: TLC for a 1906 10/12hp
Coventry Humber from a rather
diminutive chauffeur outside the
motor house. The gardener also
seems to have got in on the act.
(The Humber Register)

Opposite, top: A pleasant close-up
of one of the Humber V-twin
machines. Sam Wright, as ever,
holds the bike, while Bert Yates,
another works rider, is holding a
tool roll beside the front wheel.
(N. Portway)

Opposite, bottom: Mr A.B. Sayce
takes delivery of this sparkling
new Rudge-Multi from the garage
that supplied it, 1912.

Here a 1906/7 Argyll is taken in hand by various members of the owner's family. The car was registered FE 265, a Lincoln registration. *(Captain J. Aston RN)*

Here a 12hp Coventry Humber of about 1908 receives some attention from the family. The straw-hatted gentleman on the right makes use of a Humber oil can. *(The Humber Register)*

The cold of this January morning in 1908 is almost palpable and one cannot but admire the lady at the wheel of this 30hp Beeston Humber. She seems warmly clad but there is no screen or other weather protection. A 15hp Coventry Humber is just visible in the gateway. The location is Cassiobury Park, Watford. (*B.K. Goodman*)

The shooting-brake or estate-wagon was an essential part of any sizeable country property. Here is a Lorraine-Dietrich, one of the very many cars owned by Lady Carvely of Harlow. (*E. Salisbury/ J.C. Tarring*)

Another example of the Lorraine-Dietrich make, this landaulette is immaculately turned out. It boasts a fine set of lamps and an Autovox horn. The white-coated chauffeur responsible for the car could be well pleased by his efforts. *(H.A. Buttery)*

This impressive chain-driven Napier, with separate hoods for front and rear compartments, includes a perky little dog among its passengers. *(D. Irvine)*

Rather akin to Birmingham Small Arms (BSA) in this country, the Liège company Fabrique Nationale d'Armes de Guerre was a vast armaments company that also produced high-quality motorcycles and cars. This example dates from about 1910.

Despite the summer sunshine, the occupants of this Clement-Talbot are well wrapped up for their trip into the country. The tubular object on the running-board is an exhaust whistle. Controlled by a lever or pedal, it allowed the exhaust gases to sound a warning of approach.

A splendid shot of the business of wheel changing, in this case on a Clement-Talbot of about 1913. The chauffeur gets on with the job while my lady remains seated. The state of the road surface shows why such troubles were common.

Opposite, top: There is no explanation as to how this disaster happened to a large Mercedes. One may only hope there were no human casualties. *(Midland Automobile Club)*

Opposite, bottom: The heavens must have opened on 21 August 1912 when this 1910 10/12 Coventry Humber, owned by H.M. Lloyd of Llanwrda, tried to negotiate this flooded road. *(Lynn Hughes)*

In 1911 the Prince Henry Trial, already well established as a continental event, also came to Britain. Here, at Hereford on 11 July of that year, Prince Henry's white Benz heads the line, followed by the Duke of Connaught's Daimler saloon, as the crowds pack round. *(Bustin, Hereford)*

Opposite, top: Princess Mary visits Ludlow, Shropshire, in July 1909. Daimlers were almost invariably chosen as the royal cars, giving a considerable cachet to the make. *(Ludlow Museum)*

Opposite, bottom: Crowds of loyal supporters and sightseers turned out to greet the royal Daimlers at Wigan on 10 July 1913. Note the royal arms displayed centrally above the screen and the customary absence of a registration number on the royal car.

This Ford Model T provides transport for the Bishop of Grantham, in top hat, and other clerics on an ecclesiastical occasion, 7 July 1913. *(M. Crosthwaite)*

Opposite, top: A simple country wedding in rural Herefordshire, *c.* 1909. The cottage in the background was the bride's home, now decorated with a few Union Jacks. The car hired for the occasion has been decorated with garlands of real flowers. *(Bustin, Hereford)*

Opposite, bottom: A 2-cylinder Napier, almost certainly a hire car and suitably bedecked, awaits this wedding party. Its registration number is that of the City and County of Dublin, so it may be that the location is an Irish one.

Algernon Lee Guinness at the wheel of a Darracq in the grounds of his home in Datchet, near Windsor. On more serious business his Darracq was of a very different complexion . . . *(S. Hall)*

. . . the formidable 200hp racing Darracq with which he put up a speed of 120.26mph over the flying kilometre at Saltburn in 1909. It was at the time the world's fastest, but as it was in one direction only it didn't qualify for the world record. Guinness described this car as 'an extremely hard car to handle, and a dangerous one, owing to the short wheelbase, thin frame, light front axle and the fact that the engine had never been tried out on a test bed'. *(S. Hall)*

Shelsley Walsh, Britain's longest-lived speed event. Pictured at the start of the 'closed' event on 13 July 1907 is no. 40, a 10hp Allday driven by Litchfield Meek, whose time was 266.4s. Behind him are G. Bird's 30/35 Ariel and G. Patterson's 24hp Minerva. *(Robert Cooper)*

At the same event we see the 40hp Napier entered by S.F. Edge and driven by Sydney Smith, who climbed the hill in 92.6s. *(Midland Automobile Club)*

Fromes Hill near Ledbury, Herefordshire, attracted a big entry for the hill-climb held there in 1907. Here a 24/30hp Mass tackles the hill where there was no protection for spectators. *(J. Ahern/D. Irvine)*

This car, thought to be one of the 1908 1208cc Isotta-Fraschinis, closed the road prior to the Herts MCC's hill-climb on 3 May 1913 at Kop Hill, Bucks.

This large handsome Darracq of about 1910 has paid a call at the Hop Pole Hotel at Bromyard, Herefordshire. For a game of billiards, perhaps? *(J. Strickland)*

This Daimler landaulette poses outside the Hotel Metropole, *c.* 1909. The lamps are shrouded in covers to keep them clean when not in use.

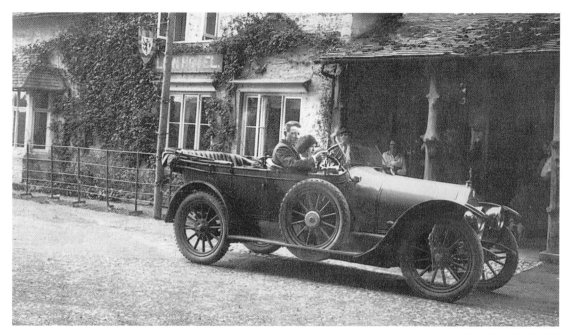

A 14hp Darracq of 1914 is about to move off after patronising the Lion Hotel in Leintwardine, Herefordshire. *(Leintwardine Local History Society)*

An air-cooled 2-cylinder Humberette cyclecar stands outside the Bowling Green Hotel at Hadley, Worcestershire. This little car and its owner were frequent visitors to local pubs.

Cars of this general design, in which the driver, usually a chauffeur, sat over the engine, provided a short wheelbase vehicle that was very handy in town traffic. Both car and chauffeur are very smartly turned out, as is the young lady seen alighting. *(R. Howard)*

This resplendent 16/20 Sunbeam landaulette of about 1912 is well matched by the chauffeur alongside. Note the leather sleeve beneath the off-side front spring, used to house the starting-handle grip. *(R. Cookson)*

Left: The chauffeur stands beside this Star of about 1909. Much of a chauffeur's time was spent waiting for his employer. *(R.J.R. Benson)*

Below: This chauffeur must indeed have been very proud of his magnificent charge, a Delaunay-Belleville equipped with very large balloon tyres. Perhaps he has been ordered just to take the dog for a drive! *(J. Pratt)*

Opposite, top: Wolseley-Siddeleys were popular in Hereford in Edwardian times, as witness this immaculately turned out example of about 1907. *(Bustin, Hereford)*

Opposite, bottom: A discerning gentleman's motor cars are seen here at Neuadd Fawr, Llandovery, in about 1913. On the left are two sleeve-valve Daimlers alongside a very sporting 'Alfonso' Hispano-Suiza. One can only admire the owner's taste! *(Carmarthen RO)*

Right: The Ludlow Motor Garage, *c.* 1907. Argyll CJ 177 is in the doorway. Tyres are much in evidence. Note the CTC (Cyclists' Touring Club) plaque on the wall. *(D. Lloyd/J. Wood)*

Below, right: Inside the same premises, with the same Argyll centre-stage. AWD 1 and AWD 2, seen on the right and left, were Shropshire trade plates. *(D. Lloyd/J. Wood)*

Below: Builth Motor Garage, Breconshire, *c.* 1907. To the right is a 1906 10/12hp Coventry Humber and behind it a Minerva of the same year. *(Brecon Museum)*

Advertising posters adorn the walls in the interior of this Malvern garage. The white car, Y 14, is a Beeston Humber, and the chassis awaiting a body is a Model T Ford. *(F.S. Banford)*

Here at Guisborough Hall, Yorkshire, is an impressive line of Delaunay-Bellevilles. From left to right are LE 4553 of *c.* 1910, LK 4535 with electric lighting of *c.* 1913 and LB 3850 of *c.* 1907, all London registrations. *(Photograph reproduced by courtesy of Kirkleatham Museum, Redcar)*

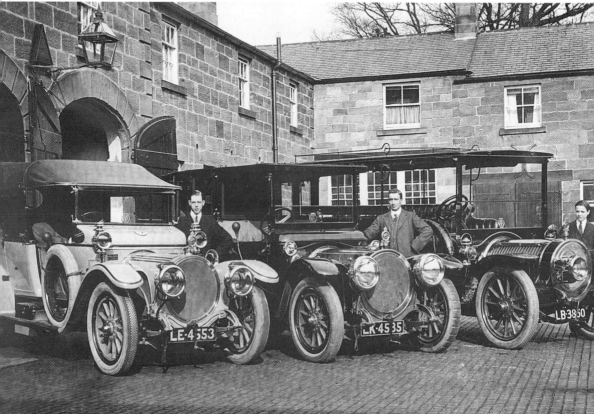

This Edwardian Clement-Talbot is housed in close proximity to the loose-boxes and poultry in this amusing domestic scene.

The Corve garage in Ludlow, Shropshire, was opened in 1917, about the time of this photograph. Outside is a rare American car, a Briscoe, easily recognisable by its single 'cyclops' headlamp. The Ford Model T inside has wartime masked headlamps. *(D. Lloyd)*

This is the 4-cylinder Hutton driven by W. Watson to win the 1908 'Four-Inch' TT in the Isle of Man. At this time Napiers were avidly promoting 6-cylinder cars, so this machine and two team-mates were entered as Huttons. This car still survives. *(J. Pratt)*

Watson's Hutton at full speed, alarmingly close to the packed spectators at the side of the road. His winning speed was 50.25mph.

The Humber team for the 1914 TT in the Isle of Man pictured at their HQ, the Mitre Hotel at Kirk Michael. Left to right: no. 13, W.G. Tuck (standing extreme left); no. 20, Sam Wright; no. 2, F.T. Burgess. Also present are some of the riding mechanics and several (mostly female) members of the hotel staff. *(N.W. Portway)*

Richard Lisle with one of the two Stars entered for the race, in which both cars were out of luck. Here we see Lisle's mechanic having to 'get out and get under' before the Stars went out on the fifth lap. *(Miss M. Burgess)*

A 25.5hp Talbot driven by Leslie Hands at Saltburn, 1914. His speed was a very creditable 103.55mph. *(Photograph reproduced by courtesy of Kirkleatham Museum, Redcar)*

One of the hazards of racing on sand was the possibility of being bogged down. The car in trouble here is a Metallurgique, while behind it may be seen a Prince Henry Vauxhall and what looks like another Metallurgique saloon. *(Redcar & Cleveland Museums Service)*

W.G. Tuck, a Humber works driver of note, with one of a series of special racing models in which he took many records in the 11hp and 14hp classes. Filling the radiator is Bert Yates (arrowed), who had made his name some years earlier with Humber motorcycles. (*L.K. Tavinor*)

Among the sixty or so cars that Lionel Martin owned over the years was this fine Vauxhall 30/98, chassis E8. The body shown here was fitted in October 1916. This picture at Brooklands dates from 1917. (*Martin Henley/Addis Collection*)

Bucking bronco! Handel Davies finds his 3hp James a bit of a handful at the Caerphilly hill-climb in 1913. History doesn't relate whether he was unseated eventually . . . probably not, as he was a very skilled rider. *(Lynn Hughes)*

Opposite, top: This big James sidecar outfit, with its swept-back handlebars and step-boards, was typical of its time. The registration is a Northumberland one, and is likely to have pre-dated this machine by quite a few years.

Opposite, bottom: Night start. The MCC Jarrott Cup Trial, 22 March 1913. Here is J. Dawson at the start with his Clyno combination. *(R. Abbott)*

This smart Talbot, fitted with a boa-constrictor horn and detachable rims, is pictured in the early spring of 1914 and captures a typically English scene in the last fragile months of peace.

Opposite, top: Rosedale Abbey Bank was a notorious ascent in Yorkshire with very steep gradients and a surface that at best could be described as appalling, but as we can see here it had bags of spectator appeal.

Opposite, bottom: This 1913 Studebaker Model AA of 27.2hp, a coupé, is unusual in having transparent panels aft of the rearwardly hinged door. It is in pristine order, and the bewhiskered driver is obviously proud of it.

The GWK, built initially in Datchet, Buckinghamshire, was a successful example of the use of friction drive, a form of transmission that was low in initial cost and overcame the bugbear of the 'crash' box. This 1913 car had a vertical-twin engine at the rear. (Mrs G. Moore)

Seen here is a rare make of cyclecar, the Averies, made by Averies-Ponette Ltd of Englefield Green, Surrey. This one was registered PA 5012 (Surrey) but was owned in Shropshire. (R.J.R. Benson)

Two shots of a
delightful sporting
12/16 Sunbeam
owned by Frank Fox
of London, but
registered as FF 272
in Merionethshire,
Wales. *(B. Dowell)*

These cars were made by the Saxon Motor Car Company, Detroit, from 1913 to 1923. Surprisingly, no fewer than 27,800 cars were produced in 1916, the firm's peak year. *(The Vintage Sports Car Club)*

The Star Hotel at Ripon, Yorkshire, is the backdrop to this picture of a 1915 Newey light car, made by Gordon Newey Ltd of Birmingham. The picture was taken by H. Mortimer Batten, who wrote on country matters in the motoring periodicals, on 13 October 1915. *(Mrs G. Moore)*

The car bidding us goodbye in the last days of peace is a Metallurgique with the London registration LL 4761. *(R.J.R. Benson)*

This Triumph motorcycle and rider are being checked at an emergency 'War Test' mobilisation control at Maidenhead, 1914. *(R. Abbott)*

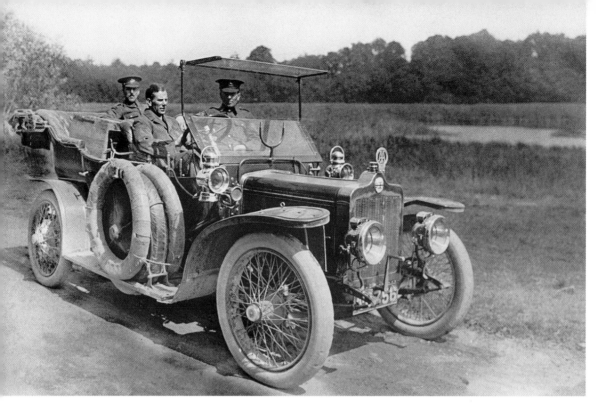

This large Edwardian Standard touring car is still in civilian ownership, despite its military passengers. Note the two wrapped spare tubes alongside the covered spare wheel and the forked lamp bracket in front of the screen. *(J. Pratt)*

Humber Ltd of Coventry took this official photograph of their smart turnout for the local British Red Cross. *(The Humber Register)*

A Mors with an adapted trade body transports these military men who do not appear to be on an urgent mission. *(J. Pratt)*

A Crossley staff car on service in a warm climate overseas, perhaps a less strenuous area than the Western Front. *(Pritchard, Hereford)*

Crossleys like these saw much active service with the armed forces in every theatre of war. *(Pritchard, Hereford)*

The soldier at the wheel of this Vauxhall staff car brought it home with him after the 1918 armistice. He had been head chauffeur to a wealthy Worcestershire gentleman who maintained a fine series of quality cars. *(R. Smith)*

What could be more suitable for a dashing young RFC pilot than this water-cooled Grand Prix Morgan as a car for a spot of leave?

But a more senior Army officer chooses a more sedate car in the form of a small Mathis, which at least boasts two handsome horns. *(The Lord Dudley)*

This large Wolseley tourer, bearing a military number on the bonnet, boasts a fine display of lights and an impressive klaxon horn. The whole outfit is typical of the larger staff cars of the time. *(J. Pratt)*

Opposite, top: Women's contribution to the war effort took many forms. This lady stands beside an RFC/RAF tender in 1918. *(J. Dearling)*

Opposite, bottom: Lieutenant-Commander W.P. Mark-Wardlaw RN, Major Goldie and the driver in Prince Arthur of Connaught's staff car, which Major Goldie had borrowed for the occasion. 'We had no breakdowns in this Vauxhall staff car and only one stoppage through punctures,' read Lt-Cdr Mark-Wardlaw's original caption. *(Captain J. Aston RN)*

Back on the home front Humber Ltd had been grumbling that they were not as productive of war material as they would have liked. However, when, with W.O. Bentley, they produced his famous aero-engine all that changed. At the wheel of this 1914 14hp Humber is F.T. Burgess, Humber's Chief Designer, whose wartime association with 'W.O.' was to reap its reward after the armistice. *(Miss M. Burgess)*

Another of the ubiquitous Crossley staff cars, this one dating from the new Royal Air Force rather than the old RFC. *(J. Dearling)*

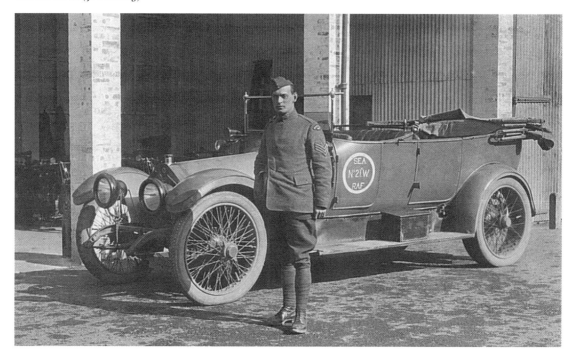

This strange-looking three-wheeler machine-gun carrier was designed by A.A. Scott of motorcycle fame. However, the military authorities were not impressed. It became the inspiration for the postwar Scott Sociable.

This 10hp Humber of 1915, with the masked headlamps of wartime, is the focus for some soldiery on medical treatment. They are wearing the blue uniform, white shirt and red tie that denoted their status. *(J. Pratt)*

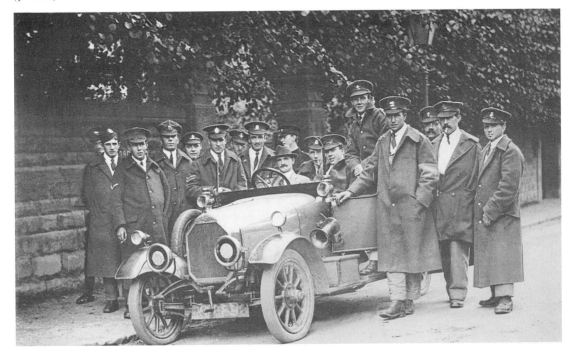

This handsome Rolls-Royce Silver Ghost with a Cheshire number is negotiating a tight corner on Hardknott with the majestic Lakeland scenery in the background on 4 August 1918. Hopes for peace to come? *(G. Summers)*

2

1919–1940

This smart Rover tourer is parked at the top of Hedsor Hill, Buckinghamshire, beside the woods that form part of Lord Astor's estate at Cliveden.

Above: Many miles could be saved by taking the ferry across the long fingers of Scottish lochs. This Prince Henry Vauxhall is on the Ballachulish Ferry. *(G.H. Taylor)*

Left: A 10hp Wolseley tourer of 1925 samples the roads and scenery in the Lake District. The original postcard bears a 1937 Cumberland postmark and the car carries a Birmingham registration.

Opposite, top: This lady driver of an AC of about 1925 again proves the popularity of the ferry as a mileage saver in the Scottish Highlands. *(C. Cottrell)*

Opposite, bottom: The front seat squab and some rugs accommodate these cheerful folk with their Maxwell tourer on the Black Mountains above Hay-on-Wye.

The sun shines, the camping gear is strewn around somewhat untidily, but our camper is enjoying a fry-up beside his Bullnose Morris. Let's hope he cleared up after himself. *(Dr W.E. Snell)*

The car is a 1922 Humber 11.4hp 2/3-seater. The nickel-plated sidelamps and headlamp rims were not a standard item on these cars. The camping arrangements include a caravan as well as a tent and seem very orderly.

You may recognise the caravan, this time being towed by a 1924 11hp Hillman with an all-weather body. At this roadside halt a 1923 8hp Humber 'chummy', owned by the same family, brings up the rear.

The services of Britain's two major motoring organisations, the Royal Automobile Club (RAC) and the Automobile Association (AA), were greatly appreciated by motorists in general. This AC has stopped beside an AA box in 1929. *(C. Cottrell)*

Sunshine, cloche hats and a fine 15.9hp Hotchkiss take in the atmosphere of the Landgate, Rye, *c.* 1927.

The owners of this 1928 9/20 Humber tourer pause to admire the view down the valley near the summit of Bwlch-y-Groes, the notorious Welsh hill that was frequently used in long-distance trials in the 1920s and 1930s. The scene is beautifully captured here. *(D.T.R. Dighton)*

A 9hp Riley of about 1929 has brought this picnic party to a gathering of some kind. The gentleman on the running-board appears to be making a rather risky-looking attempt to open a bottle with a sheath-knife! *(A.J.A. Pearson)*

This family were keen campers, keen enough to have built this light van as a simple caravan; adequate certainly, but hardly luxurious. The towing car is a 1931 M-type MG coupé, which must have had its work cut out with only 847cc to call on. *(Pritchard, Hereford)*

This 1920s Singer reposes far up a mountain track for its occupants to enjoy an undisturbed picnic.
(J. Pratt)

Opposite, top: The long, low, sleek lines of this SS II registered in London are emphasised by the height of the lady owner and her dog.

Opposite, bottom: This Morris Eight Series E is portrayed at Gretna Green in the year immediately before the Second World War.

Above: As saloon cars began to overtake open cars in popularity 'optional' fresh air was often available by means of a folding or sliding 'sunshine' roof. As this Morris Six demonstrates, the open sliding roof offered an excellent vantage point from which to enjoy the view. *(J. Pratt)*

Above, right: This sort of flood hazard may have appealed to trials riders, but this motorcyclist with his Norton prefers a more cautious method. Even so, he probably had to dry out his magneto afterwards. *(G.H. Taylor)*

Right: The driver of this Wolseley 10hp 2-seater is also cautious on the same stretch of road but is unlikely to come to any real harm. *(G.H. Taylor)*

Not the usual family car, this Alfa Romeo 6-cylinder saloon of about 1935 makes a pleasing backdrop for this late 1930s family snapshot. *(J. Dearling)*

Opposite, top: It is December 1932 and this unfortunate Bullnose Morris needs repairs to a rear spring – not a job the present-day motorist would be prepared to tackle by the roadside.

Opposite, bottom: This accident occurred at the junction of the Alton and Portsmouth roads in about 1924. The Dodge landaulette that seems to have caused the trouble belonged to Mrs Wilson-Clive, while the Talbot (XH 2889) was owned by Colonel the Hon. Angus McDonald. At the rear are a Swift cyclecar and a Ford Model T.

This small girl stands in the front compartment of an Austin 7 Ruby saloon . . .

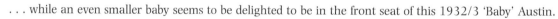

. . . while an even smaller baby seems to be delighted to be in the front seat of this 1932/3 'Baby' Austin.

Chains and cogs, or should it be chains and dogs? This family pet poses in its young master's pedal-car. (*Mrs G. Moore*)

Studied indifference: a large shaggy dog and the Alvis hare mascot, the latter on the radiator of an Alvis 10/30 of 1922, but no longer in the first flush of youth.

The Model T Ford suffered many permutations and here a sporting image is clearly the intention; that exaggeratedly long tail must at least have been robust to support the load shown here. The nearside of the bonnet has the legend '204 mph', approximately Segrave's top speed with his Sunbeam 'Slug' at Daytona. *(J. Pratt)*

Family and dog pose beside their 1930 Morris Oxford Six.

This Bayliss-Thomas 2/3-seater seems smart enough already but its lady owner and friend still like to apply more polish.

Here we see Charlie Sgonina, the 'Welsh Wizard' motorcycling ace, surveying the prospect of a lot of work – rather more of a rebuild than casual maintenance – on his sporting Fiat 509S. (*Mrs C. Sgonina*)

This Bullnose Morris 'chummy' has had a very nasty smack. The non-safety glass must have caused severe injuries. The car has been brought into a Herefordshire garage on a towing 'ambulance', one hopes for repair, but it was probably scrapped. (*F. Williams*)

This sizeable garage and showroom in Leeds is very well presented. A petrol pump flanks the entrance, in which stands a Deemster car. There is an agreeable absence of advertisements and the usual clutter that adorns such premises, which no doubt inspires confidence in any potential customers. (*Mrs G. Moore*)

New 11.4hp and 15.9hp Humbers gathered in the Final Despatch department at the Coventry Works in 1922. Only one saloon is to be seen among the many 2- and 4-seater tourers. *(The Humber Register)*

A showroom rather than a garage or workshop, portrayed here is the Humber Showroom at 32 Holborn Viaduct, London, in 1922. In front are two 4½hp flat-twin motorcycles, a touring model on the left and a sports model on the right. In the foreground is an 11.4hp tourer and behind that an 11.4hp coupé, an 11.4hp single-door saloon and a 15.9hp tourer. A wartime BR2 aero-engine right at the back is a reminder of the firm's co-operation with W.O. Bentley. *(The Humber Register)*

Left: A Norton, registration KL 7302, unusually with electric light and leg guards, takes this young man out into the heart of the country.

Opposite: The OHV flat-twin ABC was an advanced and distinctive machine designed by Granville Bradshaw. These machines were fully sprung fore and aft and incorporated a four-speed unit gearbox operated through a 'gate' change like a car. This was a major advance on the usual quadrant control used by the majority of motorcycles. *(G.S. Boston)*

Left: Plus fours, leathers, a warm scarf and a beret make this keen rider of a Norton more typical of the breed than the young man above.

Opposite: The cloche-hatted young pillion rider sits side-saddle on what was colloquially called the 'flapper-seat' of this Cornish-registered BSA.

A very smart Douglas flat-twin outfit with polished aluminium discs and two identically clad ladies is followed by a Harley-Davidson sidecar outfit. This photograph was taken in Herefordshire in the early 1920s. *(Pritchard, Hereford)*

The low build of this sporting aluminium sidecar is immediately apparent. It is coupled to a Sunbeam, which, in view of that firm's competition career, makes the registration number, a Devon one, highly appropriate. *(R. Chapman)*

This young man seems to have realised many a motorcyclist's dream in owning a big V-twin Brough Superior. It has a Kent registration. Engine no. 20990, a standard model SS80, it was owned from 11 April 1924 by J. Ayton, seen here.

The motorcycle provided an economical entry into the 'freedom of the road' for many a young man, as these Rover Scouts pictured on 23 May 1926 at Dunkery Beacon would doubtless testify. *(R. Howard)*

Here a competitor tackles the stop/start on one of the hills in the Colmore Cup Trial held in the Midlands on 24 February 1923. *(F.R. Logan)*

An atmospheric shot. The smoke from the
starting gun hasn't drifted far as the rider, cap
flat-aback, starts his climb, probably at Kop Hill,
Buckinghamshire.

Red Marley near Abberley, Worcestershire, had a
fearsome gradient and was a 'freak' hill-climb.
Here Frank Williams (Sunbeam) is on his way to
a record climb on 27 June 1931. *(F. Williams)*

F.W. May, cigarette dangling from his lips, is seen here in the Colmore Cup Trial on 19 February 1927. He was awarded a silver medal. *(F.R. Logan)*

Opposite, top: The cockpit of this 1921 Rover 8hp air-cooled 2-cylinder is sparse. The Lucas switchboard for the electrics hides coyly on the right of the steering wheel with the bulb horn just beside it. *(J. Ahern/D. Irvine)*

Opposite, bottom: Simple but balanced, the dashboard of this 1919 Horstman is typical of a light car of this time. Unique, however, is the prominent kick-starter in the centre. If its operation was highly hazardous to one's shins, at least there was no need to get out of the car. *(T.H.D. Attewell)*

A typical mid-1920s open 2-seater cockpit. The polished item in the centre of the dashboard is a lidded ashtray. Maker's and dealer's plates adorn the dashboard. *(J. Pratt)*

Opposite, top: Another Rover 8 cockpit but with a difference. The rectangular box in the centre was in essence a roller over which a map could be unrolled to aid navigation on a lengthy continental trip undertaken in 1921. *(A.R. Abbott)*

Opposite, bottom: An official Humber Works photograph of 13 August 1919 showing off the cockpit of the post-war 10hp Humber. It was a simple affair with no frills, but tidily set out. There was no clock or speedometer even. The filler cap of the gravity tank protrudes through the dash. *(The Humber Register)*

The very fully instrumented cockpit of Sir Henry ('Tim') Birkin's blown 4½-litre Bentley for the Ards TT in 1930. Birkin crashed at Ballystockart on the 32nd lap.

Opposite, top: The cockpit of a closed car. A quality saloon, the 15.9hp Humber was top of the maker's range. The claw-like object at the bottom centre of the dashboard is the pull-out handle for the electric starter. *(The Humber Register)*

Opposite, bottom: The fascia of this 1924 Aston-Martin shows a well-balanced set of instruments with a tubular dashboard lamp to light up the clock and speedometer. The Lucas switchboard occupies the centre position. *(N.W. Portway)*

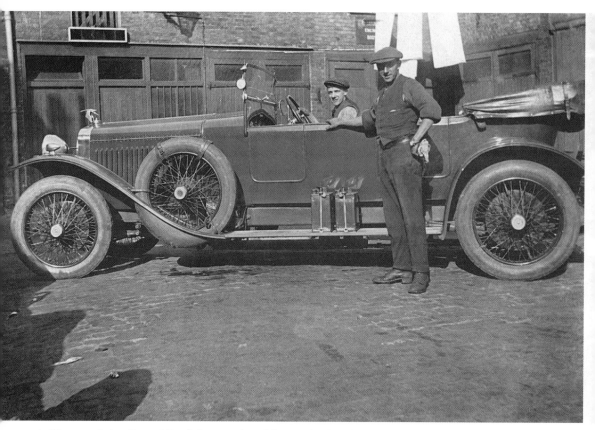

A Hispano-Suiza Type H6 of the sort loved by Michael Arlen displays the characteristic 'flying stork' mascot.

Opposite, top: Inquisitive schoolboys gather to try their luck at blowing the propeller of this AC's aeroplane mascot while the car is parked outside a garage. *(C. Cottrell)*

Opposite, bottom: This delectable Darracq tourer of the early 1920s sports a mascot portraying a young girl leaning into the wind with her arms outstretched behind her, a popular representation of speed. *(J. Pratt)*

Opposite, top: One may question the appeal of the fashions of the time (*c.* 1928) as bridesmaid and page descend from an Essex sedan of the period.

Opposite, bottom: The wedding guests gather in full fig to bid their adieus after the ceremony in about 1935. An Austin, a Daimler and a Brocklebank Six saloon are among the waiting cars.

Right: The running-board of a car cannot often have been chosen as a seat to pose a newly christened baby, so proudly held by its mother here in about 1925.

Below: The bunting is out (though quite why the Japanese national flag is so prominent is hard to say) and hats are raised and cheers ring out as the Prince of Wales (later and briefly King Edward VIII) rides in a Sunbeam on a tour of inspection in Wolverhampton in 1922. *(Mrs Scott)*

Opposite, top: A more intimate occasion, this. A lucky lady is being congratulated as the winner of a brand-new Bayliss Thomas touring car, seen on the right, in about 1923.

Opposite, bottom: A pristine sleeve-valve Daimler with formal coachwork stands beside dignitaries and officials at this civic occasion. Note the contrasting degrees of tread on the front tyres. *(Mrs Scott)*

Right: The birth of a legend. Count 'Lou' Zborowski and Clive Gallop bring monster aero-engined 'Chitty-Chitty-Bang-Bang' to Brooklands for the first time on 28 March 1921. *(Martin Henley/Jack Addis Collection)*

Right: A 12/40 supercharged Mercedes undergoing tests in chassis form at Brooklands, a facility greatly valued by the motor trade. *(J. Pratt)*

Captain G.E.T. Eyston's racing career was long and varied. Here is what might be termed a racing London bus, the Safety Special, powered by an AEC diesel bus engine. Eyston took records with this bus at Brooklands on 27 October 1933. *(Mrs E. Elwes)*

Opposite, top: W.G. Barlow took delivery of his new sports Aston-Martin in February 1923, when this picture was taken at Brooklands. *(G. Simpson)*

Opposite, bottom: This is the RLB, consisting of a Bugatti chassis with a side-valve Aston-Martin engine. R.L. Barrett raced it at a Surbiton MC event at Brooklands on 2 July 1927, and J. Crickmay followed suit on 28 May 1928, when it was painted cream with red wheels. *(G. Simpson)*

The single-seater Duesenberg driven by Duller in the 500-Miles Race of 1935 is seen here before the start. A Bugatti is alongside and Talbot, Railton and Riley spectators' cars form the background. (*Walter Gibbs*)

Brooklands was an aviation centre as well as a racetrack, as illustrated here in about 1935. The biplane is only a few feet above the speeding cars. (*Walter Gibbs*)

Racing comes to London. The ERAs of (left to right) Mays, Fairfield, Whitehead and Dobson line up at the Crystal Palace for the Coronation Trophy, 1937. *(D.P. Brogden)*

With the backing of their government the German racing teams of Auto Union and Mercedes-Benz hit the continental racing scene in 1934 and soon showed their superiority. The first time they were seen in the UK was at Donington Park in 1937 for the British Grand Prix. Here the Mercedes-Benz of Manfred von Brauchitsch is seen lining up for practice with one of the sadly outclassed ERAs in the background. No one who watched the race could fail to be bowled over by the sound and fury and efficiency of the German cars. *(D.P. Brogden)*

This lady driver's husband, Trubie Moore, was an avid and regular competition motorist in Yorkshire and the north of England. The car is a 12hp Palladium which took the family on a lengthy tour of Wales in 1923. *(Mrs G. Moore)*

Violette Cordery put up many sporting successes when driving for Invicta, long-distance records being her particular forté. She is at the wheel in this night shot in the pits at Monza, Italy, during a record bid. *(Edward Mills)*

The lady at the wheel is believed to be the Hon. Dorothy Paget, financial sponsor of Birkin's 'blower' Bentley project, just after achieving 114mph on the road in this big Mercedes-Benz. *(C. Cottrell)*

Lady drivers were not always what they seemed. Competing in the Mannin Moar on the Isle of Man in 1934 is Vasco Sameiro with an Alfa Romeo, seen here giving a treat to two lady members of the hotel staff. *(C. Cottrell)*

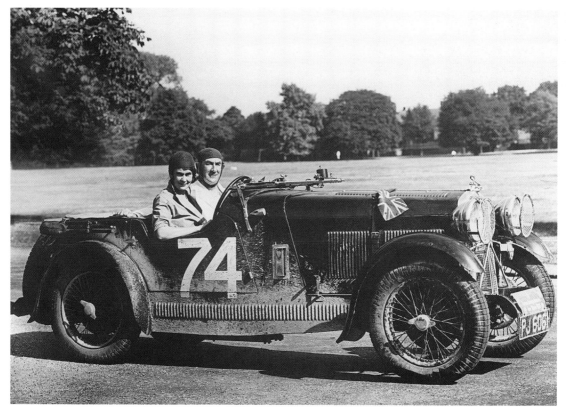

A rare car at Shelsley Walsh hill-climb on 5 May 1928 is this 1372cc Sage-engined HNT driven by H.V. Cooke. He had only one run and achieved a time of 61.2s. *(Midland Automobile Club)*

Opposite, top: Mrs Agnes Gripper, in dark overalls, with the Frazer Nash she drove in the 1933 Alpine Trial. Both she and her husband were prominent with this make in the 1930s. *(A. Gripper)*

Opposite, bottom: After the demise of Lionel Martin's original Aston-Martin firm in 1925, he devoted himself assiduously to administrative duties in the sport. Later his wife Kate, seen here driving a Wolseley Hornet in the Alpine Rally of 1934 with Lionel beside her, took an active part in competition. *(J. Martin)*

Getting there! The white Invicta 4½-litre is on tow behind one of the lorries belonging to T.W. Mays & Sons Ltd. On the back of the lorry, sheeted, is the Vauxhall-Villiers on the way to Shelsley Walsh in 1932. *(R. Chapman)*

The Mays Invicta stripped for action. Some idea of the popularity of this event may be gained from the crowds. *(R. Chapman)*

John Bolster's home-built 'Bloody Mary', a very potent Shelsley Special, is pictured at the top paddock by the finish on 3 September 1932. His times were 49.2 and 48.8s. *(M. Crosthwaite)*

Oil! Earl Howe (left, in cap) and Leslie Wilson, MAC Secretary (centre), attend to an oil spillage on the track at the Esses at Shelsley, 1935. *(Midland Automobile Club)*

Above: A.F.P. Fane and helpers with his Frazer Nash at the Shelsley September 1932 meeting. In 1937 Fane (in a different car) broke Mays' long sequence of records by achieving a record of 38.77s. *(M. Crosthwaite)*

Right: Whitney Straight brings his Maserati up the hill at Shelsley in appalling weather conditions on 29 September 1934. His times were 44.6 and 44.2s. *(Mrs A.G. Gripper)*

Opposite, top: One of Shelsley's immortals: E.J. Moor with 'Wasp I' seen on the start line on 3 September 1932. This was a typical Shelsley Special. *(M. Crosthwaite)*

Opposite, bottom: September 1932 again, and here R.H. Eccles is being pushed up to the start in his Frazer Nash no. 33. *(M. Crosthwaite)*

This rare 2LS Ballot is paying a call at an inn in the Lake District. Registered YA 3717, it was being driven here by Henry Spurrier of Leyland fame. It had been supplied new to R.J. Fry of Bristol on 30 June 1922. *(Mrs U. Parker)*

Still in the Lake District, a smart 12/50 Alvis tourer waits in the sun on a hot summer day while its owners refresh themselves at the Royal Oak Hotel, Keswick, in about 1926.

The Beach Hotel at a northern venue attracts a group of happy holidaymakers with a Hurtu of about 1921. *(Mrs G. Moore)*

A fine assembly of vehicles including bullnose and flatnose Morrises and even a steam wagon (far right) pictured outside the picturesque Cat and Fiddle Inn in the New Forest.

An informal gathering of visiting Yorkshire motorists at the Dun Bull, Mardale, in March 1925. Examples of Bullnose Morris, Horstman, Talbot and Darracq cars are visible. The Dun Bull was later demolished, along with the villages of Mardale Green and Measland, during the construction of the Haweswater Reservoir. The valley was flooded in 1935, and the Haweswater Hotel was built beside the reservoir, to replace the Dun Bull. (*Mrs G. Moore*)

A 14hp Rover tourer with a Gloucestershire number (AD . . .) and a 16hp Sunbeam await their owners' pleasure outside the Bear Hotel, Rodborough, Gloucestershire.

A bevy of Austins that had taken part in the MCC London–Land's End Trial in 1936 stand outside one of the best-known and most photographed hostelries in the UK. *(A.B.I. Dick)*

Barbara Skinner, the future Mrs John Bolster, of the Skinner family of SU carburettor fame, was an experienced racing motorist. She is seen here at the wheel of her Skinner Special of Morris Minor ancestry at a speed trial, probably at Lewes, where she competed in 1934 and 1936.

This New Hudson three-wheeler registered FK 1417, a Worcester city number, is portrayed at the Madresfield Speed trials on 22 June 1922. The car's owner was Lieutenant J. Kettle. *(J. Pratt)*

Opposite, top: Major W.H. Oates brings his slim single-seater Lagonda up Chatcombe Pitch, Gloucestershire, in 1921. *(G.S. Boston)*

Opposite, bottom: A.G. Gripper's 12/50 Alvis portrayed here in a typically rugged section of the Scottish Six Days' Trial, 1926. *(Mrs A.G. Gripper)*

A wonderfully evocative scene as a Morgan heads the line at the Llangennech hill-climb in the wilds of Wales, 1920. *(Lynn Hughes)*

E.R. Hall with the Aston-Martin 'Razorblade', now with Rudge wire wheels, leaves a trail of dust as he speeds up Kop Hill, Buckinghamshire, in 1924. Spectators are perilously close to the road. *(J. Martin)*

An essential preliminary to a speed trial was the weighing in of the cars. Here Captain Trubie Moore, with his hand on the steering wheel, waits with friends for the reading to show at Greenhow hill-climb. *(Mrs G. Moore)*

Greenhow again, with Eddie Hall's Bugatti putting in some very impressive corner work. (*Mrs G. Moore*)

The Tourist Trophy races in Ulster were initiated in 1928 and continued on that circuit until 1936. Here Sir Henry Birkin's 8-cylinder 2336cc supercharged Alfa Romeo is by the pits on 22 August 1931. He crashed at Comber on the 29th lap. (*W.G. Norris*)

The year 1936 saw the demise of the pre-war Ards circuit. Portrayed that year are H.J. Aldington's Frazer Nash BMW which finished ninth overall and . . .

. . . E.R. Hall bringing his Bentley through the streets to finish in second place. He drove non-stop for the whole race. *(D.P. Brogden)*

Rallies were popular in the 1930s. The motoring itself was not particularly strenuous and prizes were often awarded for *concours d'élégance* and coach work. Often held in popular or fashionable seaside resorts, these events were social occasions as much as motoring ones. Here Handel Davies, ace racing motorcyclist and Welsh garage proprietor, poses with his daughter beside his Hillman Aero-Minx entry of 1934/5. *(Lynn Hughes)*

The owner of this 30/98 Vauxhall hailed from Cheshire, hence the registration MB 8175. They regularly made extensive continental tours each summer. Here the Vauxhall is seen near the battle-scarred fields of Verdun, scene of so much carnage during the First World War. *(G.S. Boston)*

Top: The cars portrayed in this sequence of photographs, two Vauxhall 30/98s and a 3-litre Bentley, took part in an extended continental tour in the 1920s. The magic of the mountain scenery is well captured here, as are some of the major hazards, such as overheating on the long alpine passes and the complexities of hoisting the car in a cradle from dockside to ship or vice versa in the days before ro-ro ferries. The first of the group shows one of the Vauxhalls on the Stelvio Pass . . .

Centre: . . . and in close-up . . .

Left: . . . while here the Bentley makes use of handy supplies to remedy the problem of overheating.

This Vauxhall, chassis OE 99, registered NX 5080, a Warwickshire number, is seen here on the Furka Pass . . .

. . . while its sister car, ER 807, is on the cradle ready to be hoisted aboard at Boulogne.
(All photographs: G. Summers)

This 18hp inlet-over-exhaust 4-cylinder Essex carries a Worcestershire mark as AB 7661. It was much travelled and is seen here in Switzerland during a Swiss tour.

Further afield this time, as this picture is believed to have been taken in Ceylon. It shows typical 'empire builders' with a mixed bag of cars. On the left is a very handsome 25/50 Sizaire-Berwick, in the centre a sporting GN and on the right a rather prosaic Overland. *(J. Pratt)*

This fine D8 Delage saloon, seen in Menton,
is on tour in the summer of 1931.
(G.S. Boston)

Its companion on the tour was this 16/50
Humber 4-door Weymann sports coupé, here
halted to allow its occupants to admire a fine
view of the Rhone Glacier. *(G.S. Boston)*

A proud owner stands beside his 40/50 Rolls-Royce Silver Ghost tourer. Unusually the lamps are not bright-plated, though if the body colour is black they may be black nickel, or possibly enamelled as the coachwork. *(A.J.A. Pearson)*

A sister car photographed in Worcester. Chassis 54 E, registered RX 5906, it was supplied new to Eustace Palmer of the biscuit company Huntley & Palmer of Reading. The coachwork is by Mann Egerton. *(M. Dowty)*

Back to the Far East. This smart Itala sports tourer was photographed in Ceylon in about 1930.
(*J. Bayliss*)

This splendid 1929 20/65 6-cylinder Humber belonged to Prince Arthur, Duke of Connaught, who had
been a very keen motorist for many years. Note the royal emblem above the screen and the splendid
elephant mascot. (*The Humber Register*)

A very surprising car to have graced Herefordshire, we see here the majestic Bugatti Royale (chassis 41100) with the coupé Napoleon body. It is said to have been rescued from wartime incarceration in the Paris sewers and was brought to Herefordshire after the war. *(Mrs N. Butcher)*

Opposite, top: Perhaps even more surprising is that the only Bugatti Royale to be bought new by an Englishman in this country (none of them was ever supplied new to reigning royalty as had been the hope) also came to Herefordshire. This is the car, supplied new to Captain C.W. Foster, who kept it for thirteen years. It was chassis 41131, with a Park Ward 4-door limousine body. *(Mrs N. Butcher)*

Opposite, bottom: Late 1930s speed and luxury. This 1937 Lagonda LG 45 was the first of the make to embody some of W.O. Bentley's modifications. The polished aluminium wheel discs were an extra, but considerably reduced the labour of cleaning the wire wheels.

Contrasting dignity with insouciance, the Trojan was a highly unconventional economy car designed by Leslie Hounsfield. This example wears pneumatics rather than the solid tyres that were a cheaper option and is fitted with a curvaceous hard-top to its tourer body. It has also acquired a dent on the snout, but this does not worry the gentleman leaning on the car. *(J. Pratt)*

An early Bullnose Morris is the only car visible at this well-known Isle of Wight shoreline.

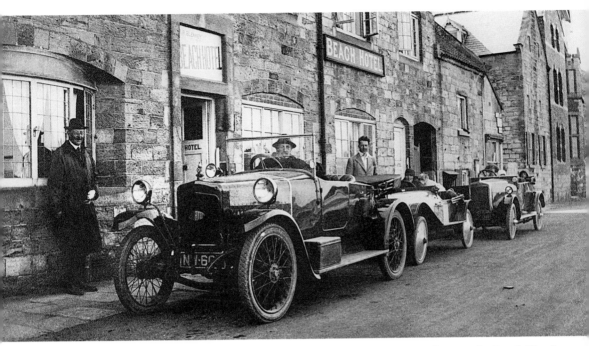

A Hurtu of about 1921, a GN and a Rhode have brought this group of holidaymakers to the Beach Hotel somewhere in the north of England. (*Mrs G. Moore*)

A fine summer's day at the Marine Drive, Westcliff-on-Sea, Essex, *c.* 1929. The paucity of traffic was remarkable at this time. To the left is parked a Speed Model 10hp Hillman of about 1922.

A Lagonda saloon of about 1934 at a seaside location, believed to be Mousehole, Cornwall. Could that be the car's owner beside the railing looking across the harbour?

Opposite, top: Two Jowetts, an Austin 7, a Rover 8 and a motorcycle take the salt air at Exmouth in the 1920s.

Opposite, bottom: Rather busier is the promenade at Brighton with a long line of landaulette taxis, among which Austins and Beardmores are visible in the foreground.

A Wolseley Nine saloon awaits the steamer, looking to Skye from Lochalsh in the mid-1930s.

Classy Torquay proves popular with its spacious and attractive gardens and promenade. Apart from the family Morris on the right, most of the cars date from the mid-1930s.

A Worcester-registered Standard 8 waits while its owner takes in the atmosphere, despite the No Parking sign.

Every schoolboy's hero, Malcolm Campbell is seen here in relaxed mood as he stands beside his 350hp Sunbeam at Pendine before a record attempt in 1925. *(Lynn Hughes)*

Left: Campbell's rival at Pendine was Parry Thomas, whose aero-engined 'Babs' is pictured at Thompson and Taylor's Brooklands premises in 1926. Beside the car is 'Buddy' Taylor. As is well known, Thomas was killed in the car in 1927 during a land speed record attempt. *(C. Cottrell)*

Below, left: Sandy beaches were popular for sand-racing, though they took a heavy toll on machinery. Here Miss Victoria Worsley is seen on 5 July 1928, possibly at Skegness Sands. *(The Jowett Car Club)*

Opposite, top: Major Ropner's Vauxhall 30/98 'Silver Arrow' was a fine performer and is seen here at Saltburn in 1923. *(Photograph reproduced by courtesy of Kirkleatham Museum, Redcar)*

Opposite, bottom: A busy scene at Southport Sands in September 1925. In the foreground is a racing Morgan driven by R.T. Horton. The white car beyond it is a super-charged 'Targa Florio' Mercedes driven by Mayner. *(G.H. Taylor)*

It seems hard to credit that the owner of this potent single-seater GN racer sometimes drove it in this state from his home near Ludlow in Shropshire to the centre of Birmingham in the late 1920s. *(C. Hall)*

Opposite, top: World land speed record contender Mrs Segrave (soon to become Lady Segrave after her husband's successful bid for the record) stands beside the Irving-Napier 'Golden Arrow' at Daytona. This was considered by many to be the most beautiful of all the WLSR cars. *(M. Haworth-Booth)*

Opposite, bottom: Captain G.E.T. Eyston drove MGs successfully on many occasions and here we see him with the 'Magic Midget' at speed on Pendine Sands in South Wales. *(The Lindsay Collection/Lynn Hughes)*

Not pink ones, one hopes! No wonder this Norton rider looks astonished.

Opposite, top: A rather amateurish bit of publicity for the new 1½hp Villiers-engined Excelsior in 1923. Exceptionally 'fat' (left) and 'tall' riders are about to demonstrate the machine's abilities.

Opposite, bottom: Motor cars often took part in carnivals and the like, frequently in support of worthy causes. This purports to be HMS *Excelsior* but is in fact a Bayliss Thomas light van. The name was probably chosen because the same firm made Excelsior motorcycles.

Opposite: This very strange-looking three-wheeler appears to have been home-built, but to a higher standard than many. Suspension seems non-existent and the choice of water-cooling is unusual for so simple a project. *(J. Pratt)*

Right: A hole in a hedge left by George Dance, Sunbeam's ace motorcycle sprinter, when he had a nasty surprise and 'lost his brake' at a speed hill-climb at Cat's Ash near Newport in South Wales. Faced with a corner he couldn't possibly take at his speed, he opted for a 'soft' hedge and found himself plunged head-first into an orchard, fetching up with an apple bough wrapped around him. Although shaken, he suffered no serious damage. *(Mrs J. Romsey)*

Below: By 1939 the shadow of war loomed. This Singer coupé (on trade plates) shows the compulsory headlamp mask and white edges to the running-boards imposed before private petrol stopped entirely.
(M.W.N. Bancroft)

Left: A young member of the Home Guard ('Dad's Army') in uniform leans on this Standard 8 with Worcester city registration.

Below, left: The same young man, apparently unarmed, 'somewhere in Worcestershire'.

Opposite, top: This Morris Eight tourer finds a little peace in 1940. Note the headlamp masks to comply with the regulations.

Opposite, bottom: One operative and masked headlamp on the near side and white paint on the dumbiron apron: all regulation wartime wear for this T-type MG in Kent.

Before the days of powered car-washes, the local river was very handy. Here an Austin Big Seven with the usual wartime restrictions is treated to a wash and brush-up at Leintwardine in Herefordshire. *(Leintwardine Local History Society)*